Bugs in My Yard

DRAGONFLIES

Kim Thompson

TABLE OF CONTENTS

A Pelican Book

Teaching Tips for Caregivers and Teachers:

Research shows that one of the best ways for students to learn a new topic is to read about it.

Before Reading

- Read the title and predict what the book will be about.
- Read the "Words to Know" and discuss the meaning of each word.
- Read the back cover to see what the book is about.

During Reading

- When a student gets to a word that is unknown, ask them to look at the rest of the sentence to find clues to help with the meaning of the unknown word.
- Motivate students with praise and encouragement.

After Reading

- Discuss the main idea of the book.
- Ask students to give one detail that they learned in the book.

Sight Words

a
away
big
by
can
eat
find
fly
have
little
what
you

Words to Know

ants

dragonfly

eyes

pond

wings

What can you find by a **pond**?

pond

You can find a little **dragonfly**!

dragonfly

Dragonflies have big **eyes**.

eyes

Dragonflies have **wings**.

wings

Dragonflies can eat **ants**.

ant

A dragonfly can fly away!

Index

Written by: Kim Thompson
Design by: Under the Oaks Media
Series Development: James Earley

Photos: Darkdiamond67: cover; JasperSuijten: p. 5; Costea Andrea: p. 7; Lorraine Hudgins: p. 9; Michael Reilly: p. 11; Claudio Carra: p. 13; Peter Ganaj: p. 15

Library of Congress PCN Data
Dragonflies / Kim Thompson
Bugs in My Yard
ISBN 978-1-63897-426-0(hard cover)
ISBN 978-1-63897-541-0(paperback)
ISBN 978-1-63897-656-1(EPUB)
ISBN 978-1-63897-771-1(eBook)
Library of Congress Control Number: 2021953295
Printed in the United States of America.

Seahorse Publishing Company
www.seahorsepub.com 1-800-387-7650

Published in the United States
Seahorse Publishing
PO Box 771325
Coral Springs, FL 33077